PLATFORM PAPERS

QUARTERLY ESSAYS ON THE PERFORMING ARTS

||||||||||||||||||||||||||||||||||

No. 21
July 2009

CURRENCY HOUSE

PLATFORM PAPERS
Quarterly essays from Currency House Inc.

Editor: Dr John Golder, j.golder@unsw.edu.au

Currency House Inc. is a non-profit association and resource centre advocating the role of the performing arts in public life by research, debate and publication.

Postal address: PO Box 2270, Strawberry Hills, NSW 2012, Australia

Email: info@currencyhouse.org.au   Tel: (02) 9319 4953
Website: www.currencyhouse.org.au   Fax: (02) 9319 3649

Editorial Board: Katharine Brisbane AM, Dr John Golder, John McCallum, Martin Portus, Greig Tillotson

Television: What Will Rate in the New Tomorrow? copyright © Ian David, 2009

ISBN 978-0-9805632-1-4
ISSN 1449-583X
Typeset in 10.5 Arrus BT
Printed by Griffin Digital

This edition of Platform Papers is supported by the Keir Foundation, the Greatorex Foundation, Neil Armfield, David Marr, Joanna Murray-Smith and other individual donors and advisers. To them and to all our supporters Currency House extends sincere gratitude.

Contents

AVAILABILITY *Platform Papers*, quarterly essays on the performing arts, is published every January, April, July and October and is available through bookshops or by subscription. For order form, see page 60.

LETTERS Currency House invites readers to submit letters of 400–1,000 words in response to the essays. Letters should be emailed to the Editor at info@currencyhouse.org.au or posted to Currency House at PO Box 2270, Strawberry Hills, NSW 2012, Australia. To be considered for the next issue, the letters must be received by 14 August 2009.

CURRENCY HOUSE For membership details, see our website at: www.currencyhouse.org.au

Television

What Will Rate in the New Tomorrow?

IAN DAVID

The author

IAN DAVID grew up in Perth and moved in 1980 to Sydney, where he graduated in screenwriting and direction from the Australian Film, Television and Radio School in 1984. He is best known for his ground-breaking reality-based dramas *Police State*, *Police Crop* and *Joh's Jury* for the ABC. In 1995 he wrote the two-part mini-series *Blue Murder*, about police corruption in NSW, which received the 1996 Logie Award for Most Outstanding Television Drama, AWGIE Award for Best Television Screenplay, AFI Award for Best Screenplay and a NSW Premier's Literary Award. His mini-series adaptation of the Robert Drewe memoir, *The Shark Net*, was screened on the ABC in 2003. His *3 Acts of Murder* was screeened by ABC1 in June 2009.

In 1990, Ian was invited by the Office of the United Nations High Commissioner for Refugees (UNHCR) to take part in a humanitarian mission to Bhutan. In 1997 he presented the annual Ian McPherson Memorial Lecture at the Sydney Film Festival and in 2001, he received the AFI's Byron Kennedy Award for services to the film industry. In 2003, he received a Centennial Medal from the Commonwealth of Australia for services to Australian society and film and in September of that year, represented Australian artists at UNESCO headquarters in Paris, with an address on cultural diversity. He was president of the Australian Writers Guild from 1999 to 2002 and is a Patron of the Arts Law Centre of Australia.

1

Test Pattern

Television's burden is that it's ubiquitous. It's so common to our social and cultural lives that we treat it with contempt. Often described as the poor man's cinema, radio with pictures or electronic newsprint, it is, however, more important than such a half-baked epithet implies. It watches us watching us. Fundamental to any understanding of ourselves in a modern world, it works on many and complex levels. From flogging fake gold chains on the Shopping Channel to Jacob Bronowski lifting ashes from a sodden pit inside the fence at Auschwitz, television comes at us as a conversation with the past, present and future.

At its essence, television is simply a way for people to see themselves. At its best it delivers very human promises. This is the way things are. This is the way things could be. It is a vital tool in the myth of progress and the authenticity of democracy, another part of the universal human experience, open to abuse and wonder.

For almost 80 years, television's arm has reached around the globe. Bhutan, the last country on earth to adopt television, signed on in June 1999. With each technological advance it gets harder to imagine the changes waiting to hatch, except that they will be faster, more mobile and become increasingly second nature. Whether it's free-to-air, delivered by cable, internet or mobile phones, television grows in its sophistication as a means to inform, entertain and educate. It's also a way to make money and so has to be appreciated for its diversity, as we look down the parallel but often diverging paths of public and commercial broadcasting. Whether we see it as Huxley's soma or as Eisenstein's baby carriage of revolution, it's impossible to think of modern life without television.

2

Television Revisited

Television was invented at least twice. An electromechanical system, patented by John Logie Baird, was the first system to work reliably. It was used by the BBC in the first ever public broadcast on 6 September 1929. Those broadcasts were beamed to London retailers on the afternoon of that day in order to catch customers on their way home from work, the idea being that stimulated sales would help get the medium on its feet. The first pictures were of a little light opera. Sales were slow. Baird's system was eventually discontinued in February 1937, when an all-electronic system became available.[1]

The inventor of a purely electronic means of recording, transmitting and receiving images and sound through the ether was patented in 1926, just before the Great Depression, by the Hungarian genius, Kálmán Tihanyi.[2] His system, which used cathode ray tubes and light-sensitive coatings of phosphorous to send and receive signals, attracted attention in the United States and, after a series of court battles, the patents were finally purchased by RCA in 1938, at the very time the motion-picture industry was reaching its technical and artistic zenith (with films such as *The Wizard of Oz*, *Gone with the Wind* and *Citizen Kane*). With added refinements by American inventor Philo Farnsworth, Tihanyi's system was developed by RCA in their laboratories by the Russian engineer V. K. Zworykin. After the Second World War this system was accepted as the standard and is only now giving way to technical innovations of the digital age.

On 1 July 1941, the Federal Communications Commission licensed two commercial networks, NBC and CBS, to begin transmission in New York. Six months later, when Japan invaded Pearl Harbour, the sale of television receivers was suspended. By war's end, the great divide had opened up. The Americans were deeply concerned with the commercial aspects of those little screens in every home. They saw television as a constantly revolving banner for advertising, a flickering billboard separated by chunks of variety, quiz shows or crime drama. The British attitude was very different: the airwaves belonged to the people.

From the beginning every household with a receiver was expected to buy a licence for the privilege of public broadcasting. Funded by this user-pays system, the BBC presented television as a window on the world, culturally uplifting, always striving to be fair and objective. The social and cultural responsibilities of such a position did not carry the same weight in America.

In Australia, inventors and technicians had been playing around with television since the late 1930s. When the Television Act was passed, in 1953, using radio's template of a dual-carriage system, it allowed for a public broadcaster, funded by the Commonwealth, and commercial broadcasters operating under a licensing regime regulated by the Australian Broadcasting Tribunal.

Just as the Packer and Murdoch newspapers had successfully lobbied against the ABC getting into news and current affairs until Curtin overruled their objections during the Second World War, there was extraordinary resistance to the ABC kick-starting a television service.[3] ABC technicians had been warehousing TV equipment since the early fifties. With the patronage of infrequent BBC boffins, the ABC had also gained the technical expertise to at least begin test broadcasts. But Frank Packer wasn't ready. He knew that television was going to be a force, but he was worried about the challenge of ensuring regular content, which would mean tying up distribution deals with overseas companies and attracting a loyal stable of local talent. Most of all, he was worried about TV competing with his newspapers for advertising revenue.

Once again, it was an event of national importance that forced the issue. Public opinion demanded that the Olympics be televised to the nation. Packer had delayed long enough. Professional television beamed out over Melbourne and Sydney for the first time on 16 September 1956. Then, only six weeks later, on 30 November 1956, videotape was used for the first time to transmit a newscast, *Douglas Edwards and the News*, on CBS America. Suddenly, television didn't need film anymore. It was live or it was taped. Eventually audiences would seem to overlook the difference.

With the Olympics only weeks away, Australians flooded into department stores to buy their Bush Simpsons, in time for the first broadcast, on 17 September 1956. The moment was historic: Bruce Gyngell in a shaky black and white screen uttered his stilted welcome, 'Good evening. Welcome to television.' Since then, those few murky seconds of footage that Australians regard as the birth of television in this country, have been played again and again—but the iconic moment we have been watching is in fact a sham. Gyngell's welcome was a re-enactment, recorded on 17 September 1957, when television was already one year old.[4] But as it's the closest thing we have to a genuine moment of birth, it'll have to do. Nothing beats television when it comes to verisimilitude.

The first ABC broadcast took place on 5 November 1956. It was a farce: the telecine equipment failed to work; the host, Michael Charlton, was caught in the corner of the studio dragging on a quick fag, and technicians kept kicking the lights and flats over. Things could only get better.

What developed in Australia, after the first ten years of transmission, was a robust hybrid, a rough-and-tumble struggle between the public broadcaster and the commercial networks. In the sixties, Australian television responded to its highly competitive structure. Most of the original American drama series (*Gunsmoke*, *Maverick*, *Bonanza*) came straight from the big movie studios. Shot on film and directed at the massive US market, they tapped into the vast reservoir of writers, actors and technicians hanging around Hollywood. Despite their thick-as-syrup cultural values, they looked a million dollars, because they were. They soon captured major audiences around the world. There were two reasons for that: not only did they make every other production house in the world look cheap, but they were also sold into 'territories' at bargain-basement prices. The more 'highbrow' East Coast studio-based dramas—which tended to be more 'interior', were shot on tape and 'theatrical' in content—did not reach Australia.

When the ABC and the two commercial networks, Seven and Nine, got down to feeding the transmitters, there was a critical shortage of home-grown material. The ABC preferred to source its overseas series and documentaries through the BBC, whereas the commercial networks, particularly GTN 9, relied upon American distributors and program formats. ATN 7, while building its schedule on overseas programs, was determined to work increasingly with a pool of local talent. From the outset it pursued creative endeavours with production houses such as Crawfords, a family company well established in radio programming. Little by little, Australian radio and stage actors began making the move to television. The American catalogue was infinitely seductive, but it was clear from the start that Australian viewers took a liking to seeing themselves.[5]

3

Video-Social Engineering

It's generally accepted that the Golden Age of television was the 1950s. That, of course, was the American Golden Age that gave us Paddy Chayevsky's plays, *The Honeymooners*, *You Bet Your Life*, *Sea Hunt* and *The Twilight Zone*. Most of the landmark television of that period was either celebrity-based variety, or vaudeville (starring the likes of Red Skelton, Bob Hope, or Ed Sullivan) or else high-quality video theatre. What became apparent, however, apart from the prominence of celebrities, was that television was a medium for writers. Indeed, the respect afforded them was more in line with the traditions of theatre. This was also the time when networks, particularly CBS, discovered that *film noir* techniques worked in presenting the news. Reporters should sound like detectives.

The English Golden Age arrived in the 1960s, with productions such as *Cathy Come Home, The Avengers, Monty Python, Culloden, The War Game* and the still-running *Coronation Street*. It was the 1960s that lifted television-watching into its place as the world's most popular pastime. Television sets were cheaper, better and more reliable. It wasn't just the Beatles, the Stones and popular music generally that drove the decade; television exploded. Outside broadcasts of special events, tally-room election-night broadcasts, Telethons, children's shows, live crosses and satellite feeds—they all became part of the rush of the sixties. If anything was happening, anywhere, it would be on TV.

Several events particularly stand out for me, beacons in my burgeoning appreciation of the effect television could have on me and those around me. The first took place in my early adolescence. It was a stinking hot day at the fag end of summer, when Brian Robinson went mad and became the quarry in a massive manhunt, events covered by TVW 7 in Perth. It was an unfolding drama of such intensity that all other programming was suspended. On that day, 9 February 1963, television became much more than *Dragnet, Bobby Limb* and *BP Pick-A-Box*. I remember one thing distinctly, one idea that chilled me at the time. Television is tribal. Without thought or consideration for its effects, it can manufacture an excitement that leaves strangers meeting in the street to share their common experience. It happened on that day in February.

Only two weeks before these events, serial killer Eric Edgar Cooke had gone on a shooting rampage, killing three men and firing on a couple in a parked car. When Brian Robinson argued with his father and took off with a shotgun, it was almost as though the people of Perth were expecting it.

That afternoon, neighbours had got jack of the yelling and the violent language drifting over from the Robinson household and called the cops. Constable Noel Iles knew the Robinsons. He left Belmont Police Station to drop in on them on his way home. Those long hot days at the end of summer can fray nerves, particularly since Belmont is a long way from the beach. As he approached the house, Constable Iles was shot without warning from a bedroom window. Robinson, only 23, ran out of the house, pushed Iles over with his foot and blasted him again. He ran out into the road and tried to get Andrew McDougall to give up his Goggomobil and, when he refused, shot him too. Next, Robinson forced a taxi driver to take him north and in the Gnangara Pine Plantation, 30 kilometres away, the taxi finally stopped, bogged up to its axles in the hot, grey sand. Citizens joined police in the manhunt, helping to form a cordon around the pine plantation. All night the police waited for the killer to appear and when he did, the next morning, a gun fight ensued in scrub off Widgee Road. It was as good as Ned Kelly or Ben Hall. Robinson was arrested, convicted, hanged in Fremantle Prison on the morning of 24 January 1964, and buried three hours later. He was the second last man to be executed in WA. The last was Eric Edgar Cooke, hanged on 26 October 1964.

That summer changed my perceptions about television forever. Brian Robinson set in train a series of events that was shown around the world as *Manhunt*. With their newly-acquired OB van set up on a hot road running alongside the Gnangarra Pine Plantation, it was a matter of waiting for the killer to come out. While the police decided to sit it out, the Channel 7 reporters plundered their archives, police contacts and neighbours to get the backstory. It was rivetting TV. Cut down for overseas distribution, *Manhunt* showed the world what a stakeout could do for the ratings. O.J. Simpson was thirty years away.

As the drama built over many hours, what struck me was the way in which television played at being objective, but fell in so completely with the forces of law and order. The stakeout around that pine plantation became an event, a story in the unfolding history of good versus evil. People flocked to the scene in cars and buses. This was an event, and whether they liked it or not, they were part of it. In the days following I couldn't stop thinking about the way in which the television reporters soaked up the tension and turned it into entertainment. It was made an even more heightened event by the fact that the station had assigned its OB van and reporters to this hot, unfriendly forest and turned all of us watching into players. I didn't want Brian Robinson to go free, but I was on his side. It was no longer a case of letting the police go about their dangerous work: the presence of a television crew intensified events and the chase, the stand-off, took on greater meaning. We were sick and tired of living in fear. No one knew who had killed those people two weeks ago, but maybe it had been Brian Robinson! The tribal aspect of it concerned me.

Television had brought us all together in a way that was compelling and visceral. Some of us were fearful, some of us were elated and some of us were quietly hoping for blood. All I could think of was, you wouldn't want this to turn against you.

Exactly a year after Brian Robinson's rampage, something happened that sent the world in another direction. On 9 February 1964, the Beatles made their debut on the *Ed Sullivan Show*. Richard Harrington, writing in the *Washington Post*, said it was

> a signal pop-culture moment, one of the most important events in the history of rock-and-roll and television. It was watched by 73 million people, one of the highest-rated single programs of all time, the first of three straight Sunday night appearances that would launch the stateside version of Beatlemania.

Harrington was one of many who suggested that the Beatles and television were made for each other: '[O]ver almost four decades, McCartney looked to television as the most effective, most concentrated medium to reach a mass audience.'[6]

Growing up in Perth, our AWA 21 did not have an easy life. It was on most of the time, its tuner rolled and clicked in search of a channel like a tumbler in a bank vault. It opened up the wound of our isolation, at the same time applying a soothing unguent that the world was only a channel away. When the Beatles toured in June 1964, they left Perth off their concert list. It was a savage blow. Every night, five minutes before the news, Gary Carvolth, Channel 7's baby-faced announcer, would remind us of our place at the edge of a desert with a segment called 'Beatle Tour News'. I had to take up my position directly in front of the set with my hand over the knobs, just in case my father walked in and flipped the channel. The next morning, on the way to school, all we would talk about was that precious five minutes of banished isolation.

Another event that made an equally deep impression on me was the pre-dawn screening of *Our World*, on 25 June 1967, the first live, satellite broadcast beamed to 31 countries and seen by an estimated 400 million viewers. Of the 19 countries invited, 14 contributed. Apart from Maria Callas's pitifully-short segment, the standout performance was of the Beatles cutting 'All You Need Is Love' at the Abbey Road Studios. Australia overcame enormous technical challenges to show the world some trams leaving a Melbourne depot and our elite swimmers training in a Townsville pool. It was cold and dark: the sun wasn't up. I watched the entire two-and-a-half hours, wrapped in my dressing gown, with a sense of wonder I've never quite captured since. I understood how I could be asleep and a man could be harvesting wheat in Ontario. Of course, we all know about these things, but to actually feel it is another matter. I felt I was connected to the world, to the community of human beings. Everything was connected in the here and now and I was alive. Cinema has never worked in that way for me, and neither have books.

When, in 1969, the BBC set out to tell the story of human *Civilisation* with Kenneth Clark, I was there taking notes. No school ever opened such a window into the past. Four years later, in *Ascent of Man*, Dr

Jacob Bronowski set out to describe the complex relationship between the tools of technology and the fruits of human society. In the final of thirteen episodes, Bronowski got down on his haunches behind a fence and dug his hand into the dark grey mud. This was where Bronowki had suffered deep personal loss. This was Auschwitz:

> It is said that science will dehumanise people and turn them into numbers. That is false—tragically false. Look for yourself. This is the concentration camp and crematorium at Auschwitz. This is where people were turned into numbers. Into this pond were flushed the ashes of four million people. And that was not done by gas. It was done by arrogance. It was done by dogma. It was done by ignorance. When people believe that they have absolute knowledge, with no test in reality—this is how they behave. This is what men do when they aspire to the knowledge of gods.[7]

For many people, television is the only medium of choice for news and current affairs, and there is no other way to witness major events such as a president's inauguration, the Olympics or the Tour de France. It brings the world together, and it portrays the national personality of countries fortunate enough to have both public and private broadcasters free of overbearing censorship and control. Strictly controlled in most countries under a regime of licences and boards of regulation, it's also a political tool loved and feared by those in power—or those who have ambitions to be—because of its ability to create and sustain potent messages. Where would a modern election campaign be without television? Today, in most modern democracies, the networks are legally obliged to carry major political debates, unless, of course, it's a totalitarian regime that holds the licence.

In so-called benign dictatorships, television is often used as a panacea for populations who have no choice but to trust in the strong hands on the tiller that guide their lives. From Korea to Zimbabwe, the content of a day's broadcasting is deliberately so orientated to the national 'mission' that no decent dialogue on important issues can be sustained. At the other end of the spectrum, individuals who have control of substantial media holdings can shape the world even though they don't aspire to office. For those who do aspire to office, it's a medium with enormous potential to numb down. In Italy, Silvio Berlusconi ensures that his stations persistently blunt the probing of newscasts with wall-to-wall soaps, bare-breasted quiz-show contestants and old movie replays. The message is simple: go to sleep.

In rougher political climes, where television can be a tool for fomenting insurrection, the controls are so absolute as to render worthless any message that is put out. In any coup the first installation hit is the transmitter. In his study of the use of internet and telecommunications in Africa's least Developed Countries Victor Mbarika proposed that private enterprise should be permitted much greater access to poorer African countries in order to build up their networks. He singles out countries such as Indonesia, South Africa and Egypt as examples of developing nations which have been able to build substantial telecommunications infrastructure despite their relative poverty. The developing countries 'have been able to establish high quality telecommunications services despite their poor economic conditions. This demonstrates that with a well-managed telecommunications industry, even the poorest country can have an efficient network and services'.[8] But this is true only if the political will exists. Many countries, particularly those run by despotic regimes, deliberately deny an audience access to broadcasts simply by controlling the supply of electricity to specific regions. Blackouts were common in Zimbabwe around election time.

In 1964, Marshall McLuhan suggested that the content of television programs was of minimal relevance, having all the informative illumination of 'a light bulb'. Any program would approximate the effect of any other program.[9] He suggested that it was the medium itself that exerted more influence over the sensibilities of the viewing population. His view refused to accept the cross-pollination that occurs between medium and audience in contemporary society. When those broken, fragile images of the first lunar landing arrived from space on 20 July 1969, every channel carried the pictures. In those few minutes content was everything and the medium revealed an unparalleled moment of human togetherness.

The hunt for Brian Robinson, and *Our World*, fuelled a fascination with television that I have still not lost. Every day I'm reminded of how television influences us and how we influence it. It shouldn't be so important, just a small screen in the corner with an on/off switch, a volume knob and a channel selector.

However, despite its ephemeral, almost throw-away nature, it is unassailable as the most direct expression of our immediate, collective ambition. Only our sophistication as viewers and the choice afforded proper access and resources can determine whether those aspirations are positive or not.

4

Fictional Reality

There is the dark side, of course. Whatever can be caught on camera, any image, is fodder for television. In the UK, when young James Bulger was led away on 12 February 1993, it looked like television. It had a sense of a verifiable record about it. A finality that was believable and chilling. That quality has been added to our collective appreciation of recorded history and it has undoubtedly been abused. Television is renowned for its ability to throw those shards of shocking everyday tragedy onto the screen for consumption with the family meal. By themselves those moments have that ability to deny reality, to mask the revelation. It's just someone else's tragedy.

In 2007, John Hartley suggested that television may have 'added to xenophobia, remoteness, violence and passivity. But television's textuality may also have been a site for new forms of cultural engagement and even civic participation.'[10] This touches on essential questions about how we respond to all forms of programming, but particularly to documentaries, research-based dramas and news and current affairs. However, the influence of programs such as these operates at a much deeper level than Hartley suggests. There is nothing passive about television.

One of the most important defining things about TV is that it's always on. We don't have to look up the papers, use transport and buy a ticket. We know that it's always playing. But, unlike radio, we have to find a place to watch it. Rather than being a 'passive' medium, television actively invites the audience to participate in constructing the reality they feel comfortable with, the one they most agree with. The one they want. We come to TV, then we take it with us.

When we go to the cinema we use particular resources to make a judgment about what to see. More often than not word of mouth, reviews and cast quality tend to determine our choice. The investment we make in a ticket is our responsibility. If the movie stinks, we take part of the blame for choosing to see it. It's also too late to get our money back. Television is different. After two generations of free-to-air broadcasting, we have great difficulty not seeing the content as something presented to us as a community service, a gift or a drinking fountain. If we don't like it, we can turn it off. If we really don't like it, we don't come back. Since the very beginnings of television broadcasting we have the sense that we participate not only in the program's coming into being, but also in its survival.

While films often claim to be 'true', only television documentaries are seriously regarded as 'documents of record'. A movie narrative that is 'based upon' or 'inspired by' actual events is no longer the heart-stopping event it may once have been. The emotional truth of the story, whether it is *Elmer Gantry* or *Phar Lap*, always overwhelms the alleged accuracy of the depiction. Television has a very different sensibility. It carries the news. As a medium it trades on its urgency, its immediacy. Unfortunately, television's track record is no better than that of film. In television a 'true' story is usually not.

Early on 3 March 1991, Los Angeles Police Department highway patrol officers pulled over an African-American male, Rodney King. Within a few minutes, and despite being outnumbered, unarmed and showing little resistance, King was being viciously beaten by the officers. Nine minutes of this event were recorded by one George Holliday with his new camcorder. The first minute and a half, showing the police 'subduing' King with their batons, was broadcast around the world. The beating resulted in charges against the officers, who were subsequently acquitted and exonerated.[11] The Rodney King incident was important because it showed how 'proof' of an outrage could be dismissed as irrelevant because it did not conform to the 'worldview' of a particular audience.

The Los Angeles District Attorney had an open-and-shut case: their proof was contained on George Holliday's 'untouched' videotape. The footage had been shown around the world on television. It looked 'true'. It felt 'true'. When the jury returned with acquittals for all four of the accused, it was suggested that some legal technicality had got in the way. But it hadn't. The jury chose to reject the video evidence. For them, the pictures did not reveal the truth. The reaction across America was swift: there must have been some provocation; King must have pulled a gun; the police had good cause to think he was wanted for something serious. For African-Americans it was a 'no-brainer': King was black.

Journalist Lou Cannon later revealed that the Rodney King case was much more complicated than the television pictures revealed.[12] This wasn't an open-and-shut case. The jury were shown Holliday's unedited videotape. The police brutality couldn't be excused, but it could be explained. There'd been one helluva high-speed chase; King had resisted arrest and appeared immune to two hits from a Taser. The police, using metal batons, went to work in a manner that was borderline, but not criminal. At a later trial, two of the officers, Laurence Powell and Stacey Koon, were found guilty of violating King's civil rights and served prison sentences. What George Holliday's edited footage showed was that something that looks simple isn't necessarily straightforward.

Again and again, we viewers are capable of taking in an alleged scrap of 'reality footage' of police operations, or undercover busts or current affairs stings, and accepting that those events actually happened. Why? Because that's what we want to accept. However, if we watch something that offends our sense of reality, the reality we want, we are just as capable of rejecting what we've been shown. It's been 'doctored', we say.

The context has been shifted. It's a trick of the light, smoke and mirrors. The very thought that someone has an agenda and has manipulated 'reality' is very much part of television, and ultimately television is to blame for its own lack of credibility.

Perhaps we should acknowledge that truth is a matter of opinion, that there are as many versions of the truth as there are witnesses. Ultimately, for something to satisfy everyone's version of the truth, the message has to be meaningless. In a sense, television accepts that position, anyway. Over time it's capable of presenting a multitude of angles on any particular subject. Whatever works today might not work tomorrow. What is important, perhaps more than the truth, is the intention of the messenger.

5

Clash of the Titans

The ABC has always attracted critics. My father used to write carping letters to the press about the excessive time devoted to obscure sporting events (like cricket), or the excess of plummy English accents, but he'd almost stand to attention at the kitchen table when the banner music for the midday news came on. The emerging school of aggressive journalism during the 1970s, coupled with the ABC's coverage deep into the bush, attracted closer scrutiny of its news and current affairs programming. The challenges to its boasts of high professional-ethical standards and objectivity grew louder. Investigative reporting, by its very nature, will create enemies. However, men like the Queensland Premier Joh Bjelke-Petersen—who in 1991 was put on trial for corruption and perjury, following an inquiry established in the wake of allegations made by an ABC *Four Corners* program four years earlier—saw the vigorous pursuit of his affairs as much more. For Bjelke-Petersen, criticism was proof of an entrenched and calculated bias on the part of the national broadcaster.

Nowadays, ABC-bashing seems to have become a pastime for a select group of pundits. *Sydney Morning Herald* columnist Gerard Henderson has a problem with the ABC. Sometimes. If it sails anywhere near an issue of history or politics, it usually finds itself in trouble. Too many lefties. If, however, the ABC reveals something that Henderson himself thinks needs to be outed, then he looks the other way. On 22 August 2006, he attacked the Victorian Court of Appeal for releasing Jack Thomas, who had been found guilty of terrorism charges by a Supreme Court jury six months earlier. Upholding the appeal, he wrote, served to highlight

> an emerging division within democracies. Those divisions are between the civil liberties lobby, which believes the main contemporary threat to the West turns on an (alleged) diminution of liberty, and a democracy defence lobby, which maintains that radical Islamism poses a real and present danger to Western nations.[13]

The evidence against Thomas amounted to certain admissions he had made in an interview given to the Australian Federal Police in Pakistan. The Court of Appeal ruled that, because Thomas was not permitted to have legal counsel during the interview, the evidence was not admissible.

Clearly, Henderson did not agree with the appellate judges: he was sure that Jack Thomas was guilty, because he'd made admissions to the ABC's *Four Corners* in late February 2006. He had told reporter Sally Neighbour that he had received weapons training and financial assistance from al-Qaeda and that he had on one occasion shaken hands with Osama bin Laden. Prior to this, in numerous articles, Henderson had attacked the ABC's credibility and questioned its claims to objectivity. It would appear that when the ABC supports Henderson's view, it has more credibility than the Victorian Court of Appeal. Of course, the issue isn't one of credibility, but rather the technical matter of what is or is not admissible as evidence. If the judgment is that the evidence hasn't been gathered according to the proper processes of the law, then it can't be offered to the jury to assist in their deliberations.

As to credibility, the implication of Henderson's article is that Thomas was set free by the forces of the left. In his final few paragraphs, he asserts that since it's 'fashionable in civil liberties circles to analyse the background of High Court Judges, [...] let's try the same practice with the Victorian Supreme Court. Take the Court of Appeal president, [Chris] Maxwell, for example.' He proceeds to draw his long bow and lands a shot on Judge Maxwell's history as 'a former staffer to a federal Labor attorney-general and a past president of Liberty Victoria [...] and was appointed to his present position by Steve Bracks's [Victorian] Labor Government.' What Henderson conveniently forgets to mention is that there were two other judges sitting with Maxwell. Why didn't he bother to flick through *Who's Who* and dig up the CVs of Judges Peter Buchanan and Frank Vincent? But Henderson finds his target proper in his final paragraph: 'The Thomas case outlines the division between civil libertarian types (trial lawyers, artists, humanities academics, comedians and the like) who take terrorists at their word and regard them as a genuine threat to democratic societies.'[14] One wonders if Gerard Henderson is looking in the right direction.

The ABC is never far from Henderson's crosshairs. In his *Herald* column he rails regularly at the alleged bias of the national broadcaster. One never expects to see much, if any, criticism of commercial radio or television. The opinionated get free rein—even those who have been 'bought' to speak on behalf of corporations who have the money and the inclination to fix the public mind in their favour. So, it was with some surprise that I found myself concurring with Henderson's column of 3 March this year, 'Can't See the Truth for the Screen', in which British historian Antony Beevor is quoted as saying that 'over the past dozen or so years television and movie-makers have managed to blur the border between fact and fiction to an unprecedented degree.' Beevor refers to the use of half-truths and fantasy in the 'unholy alliance between left-wing 9/11 conspiracy theorists, right-wing Holocaust deniers and Islamic fundamentalists', and goes on to denounce those who peddle fiction as fact:

> It should be the duty of not just every scientist and historian, but also of every writer, publisher, movie-maker, TV producer and ordinary citizen to fight all attempts to exploit the ignorance and gullibility of audiences. Today's silly conspiracy theory in the West can easily become tomorrow's article of faith in the world at large. Quite simply, we play with facts at our peril. From selling fiction as truth in movies to peddling the big lies of counter-knowledge is not such a very big step after all.[15]

Henderson's main target is the second series of the Nine Network's *Underbelly: A Tale of Two Cities*. Executive Producer Des Monaghan maintains that the substantial errors of fact in the series do not affect the 'overall accurate message' of the series. In response, Henderson quotes Paul Mackay, the son of murdered Griffith anti-drugs campaigner, Donald Mackay: 'I can't see how the screening of events that never occurred helps to tell the truth.' It's hard to disagree with that.

In his review of 2 March 2009, Kelsey Munro wrote that he had been assured 'by people who kn[e]w more than [he did] about the 1970s drug trade in Australia

> that *Underbelly* deviates from the strict facts. There are some arguably gratuitous rude bits and, yes, it does trade on its presumed veracity and shamelessly cash in on its actresses' bare assets, with flimsy

relevance to plot and so on. But I'll be damned if it isn't telling a ripping yarn. Fun, too, with its '70s hairstyles, clothes and decor.[16]

Two months later Munro opened his review of the final episode of the series with:

[W]e haven't seen the last of *Underbelly*. If you were in any doubt, tonight's conclusion from the cops, 'I think the war is just beginning, folks', will dispense with it. *Underbelly*'s glimpse of recent underworld history, not to mention its gratuitous boob shots, has again ensured good ratings and the third series is expected to fill the historical gap between the first two. Tonight's bloody denouement has all the requisite nudity coupled with some dodgy acting, particularly from repeat-offender Matthew Newton as Terry Clark. 'Aussie Bob' Trimbole's death-bed scene is well done until the heavy-handed hallucination of Clark returning to his side as his priest-confessor. The stylised, Tarantino-esque way the score segues into rock'n'roll every time a gun enters the frame is grating: it's murder as retro rock video. Still, *Underbelly* intrigues: I suspect it's to do with our deep desire to see local stories reflected on the small screen.[17]

This is the series that was initially touted as 'a true story' by the Nine Network's publicity department. Emblazoned across billboards and intoned at the end of numerous station promos, that simple statement promised so much. Later it was described as 'loosely based on fact'.[18] How does the audience rate that? *Underbelly: A Tale of Two Cities* mines the back catalogues of old shows and movies, skims the books and records that matter and cobbles together a form of television impressionism. The audience is entertained and the show is a success. But to insist that it is a 'true story' merely damages the audience's 'integrity antennae'. Ultimately, the *Underbelly* franchise is about success. The characters aren't even caricatures; they are criminals in a dystopian society of greed, lust and murder. Whatever they got they deserved, including a bullet. There was little to underpin the narrative drive of deals and deaths and boobs and music.

One of the writers of *Underbelly: A Tale of Two Cities* described the challenge he had with the characters:

> It was a challenge for me coming to terms with who could behave so without recourse to morality or fear. A lot of them did not feel very frightened and so getting into someone like Jason Moran's head [...] I don't think he experienced fear. Not only because I think he wasn't very bright, but because he was tough and he had that testosterone thing that clears bars.[19]

I don't know about Jason Moran, but most of the criminals I've met experience fear like any other mortal. They also get adrenaline rushes when they rob banks, but it's the fear that makes it worthwhile—like actors who can't walk out on stage unless there's a rush of stage fright.

The Mr Asia Syndicate figures prominently in *Underbelly: A Tale of Two Cities*. There were four principals in the syndicate. One of them, Chinese 'Jack' Chu, lived in Singapore. Since the show was set in Sydney and Melbourne, it's safe to assume that there wasn't much opportunity to see Mr Chu. Another, the real

Mr Asia, Martin Johnstone, also lived overseas, so he could remain scarce for the purposes of the drama. The principal who had most to do with the main character in the series, Terry Clark, was James Shepherd. He operated out of Sydney and was instrumental in bringing the syndicate together with Robert Trimbole. In fact, James Shepherd was indispensable to the operation of the sydicate. He is the syndicate's sole survivor. He is nowhere to be seen in *Underbelly: A Tale of Two Cities*. Every week, after each new episode had gone to air, Shepherd, who lives in Australia, would phone me and laugh about all the scenes he didn't have with Terry Clark.

Whether or not the audience cares for the facts isn't an issue. This second series of *Underbelly* rated its socks off, because it was sexy, well-made and very Australian. It was also rotten with historical inaccuracies. If the audience is happy to believe that Robert Trimbole distributed heroin for Terry Clark, or that Donald Mackay was murdered after the Great Bookie Robbery, or that George Freeman bashed Terry Clark or Lenny McPherson sold guns from a park bench, or Alison Dine was naïve or James Shepherd is invisible, then why should it matter? Well, it matters because they are untrue. It matters because the network, playing on the audience's justifiable expectations, is treating each and every viewer like a mug. It matters because it makes the truth a joke, a marketing ploy, another reason to view the world with a cynicism it can ill afford.

In his 3 March column, 'Can't See the Truth for the Screen', Gerard Henderson makes the point that history is contestable: 'However, it is either conceit or deceit to maintain [that] facts either do not exist or do not matter.' When writing any recreation of history, whether literary or dramatic, the research comes down to the laborious task of picking up flotsam and jetsam and piecing them together to find out what kind of boat the bits came from. The more pieces you find and the more diligence you show in putting them together, the more credible the result. Surely, there's no point in gathering all the bits to make a train, one that will drive through the ratings, and then to go and call it a boat, or at least a true representation of a boat. The Nine Network referred to *Underbelly: A Tale of Two Cities* as 'a true story'. It wasn't. The word out in the industry is that the writers were put under enormous pressure to turn out another series before the viewing frenzy cooled. Understandably, the Nine Network wanted to capitalise on the momentum of the first series. But by making such demands, the Network devalued the high regard in which the first series was deservedly held. The ratings remained high, but it had lost its shine.

6

The Mates' Club

Every media organisation has its own culture. It's a template for behaviour set down by the media baron who has the biggest appendage. Nothing better exemplifies the individual network 'personality' and the culture that supports it than the Nine Network's *NRL Footy Show*.

In May this year it was revealed on *The Footy Show* that back in 2002 one of the show's star panelists, Matthew Johns, and at least five fellow-members of the Cronulla Sharks rugby team, had been involved in group sex with a nineteen-year-old New Zealand woman. Interviewed about the incident for an ABC *Four Corners* investigative report which went to air on 11 May 2009, the woman said that the experience had left her feeling 'degraded and suicidal'.

When lust has been spent, what's left if your career's in serious jeopardy? Pain and anguish and embarrassment. Deeply uncomfortable and not his usual jokey self, Johns confessed:

> Ah, it was an incident that was investigated by police ... Ah, it caused all parties enormous pain and embarrassment ... Ah, for me personally, it put my [...] family through enormous anguish and embarrassment, and [...] for that I'm, well, you can't say sorry enough ... But the police did investigate

the situation at the time [...] and there were no charges laid, but there has been a lot of pain and embarrassment to a lot of people.[20]

Johns apologised to his family several times during his fifty seconds of pain, but his victim was only mentioned in his reference to 'all parties'. She described the night in question as 'degrading'. Johns was hurt, not for her sake, but by the 'anguish and embarrassment' of being found out and the revelation to his family that he had treated a woman as entertainment and for the perving pleasure of his team-mates.

The avuncular host, Paul 'Fatty' Vautin ended the apology with 'All right, mate, well said.' And with a light slap on Johns' back he turned to face the studio audience, adding 'All right, let's get on with the show!' The blokey culture of the Nine Network is familiar to Australian audiences. But in this instance it wasn't a case of the Network giving valuable airtime to the likes of Matthew Johns. It was protecting its investment in its high-rating show and one of its most valuable assets. Johns is the Network's creation. After a stellar sporting career he walked into a job where all he had to do was be himself. With his rough-hewn bar-room humour and a bad wig, Johns played the clown. What he does he's probably got away with at many a family barbecue. It's that kind of show.

Television made 'Matty' Johns and television would save him, or at least neutralise the damage. When the mess seeped under the door of the NRL, it was the Channel Nine managers who called in the cleaners. The fact is, the Nine Network is part of the culture, renowned for its bullish approach to business. This is a place for blokes. The Head of News and Current Affairs, Mark Llewellyn, stated that its one-time CEO, Eddie Maguire, current president of the Collingwood Football Club, casually referred to firing Jessica Rowe, one of the Network's news anchors, as 'boning'.[21] This did nothing for staff morale, but it betrayed Mr McGuire's essential purpose. He promised much in terms of programming and succeeded in delivering a lot of termination slips. Eventually, he accepted one of his own.

It was *Four Corners* who let Matthew Johns know that they intended to reveal details of the 2002 incident in New Zealand. Rugby League may have taken the hit, but it was the Nine Network who would engineer a rescue. After his *Footy Show* confession, Johns went on a holiday, obviously with the blessing of his handlers at the station. When the smell raised by the *Four Corners* report failed to clear, Johns was called back from his holiday to the Nine Network headquarters on Sydney's lower North Shore. An accommodation was hammered out: Johns would take a break, the station would issue an apology and wait for the dust to settle.

On 13 May, Johns appeared on *A Current Affair*, this time with his wife, Trish. He was guilty of infidelity and stupidity, he said, but hadn't done anything wrong. Trish was visibly distressed, but she agreed: he was only guilty of infidelity. Eventually, Johns uttered an apology to the New Zealand woman. Rugby League and the Nine Network took a big hit. In a considered and generous statement, Nine's CEO David Gyngell announced that Johns would be ceasing his connection with Nine by mutual agreement. He went on: 'I fully endorse [NRL CEO] David Gallop's comments concerning the indefensible conduct of some players and the lack of respect for women and the critical focus on all stakeholders to help eradicate it from our game. I join with him in extending my apologies and sympathy to the young woman involved in the incident, who is clearly still distressed as a consequence.'

On the 14 May edition of *The Footy Show*, veteran coach and commentator Phil Gould wept as he told players and fans that the time had come for Rugby League to fix its attitudes to women. The Johns story had been 'a sledgehammer to the back of the head'. Three days later, in his *Sun-Herald* column, Gould made this extraordinary statement:

> Players need to get the message. It doesn't matter if it's alcohol-related incidents, violence, recreational drug use or allegations of sexual misconduct; it doesn't matter how minor or even how unfounded the allegations; it doesn't even matter if you think you have the green light or even if you're positive you're 100 per cent right; chances are, it won't play out that way in the media.

What he seems to be saying is, whatever you do the media will distort, amplify or misconstrue the evidence against you. Gould makes his living as a media commentator, in print and for the Nine Network, so he should know. Again, the mates' club is exonerated. You can't win, the media will get you.

It has been suggested that television audiences won't be deprived of Matthew Johns' racy humour for long. He'll be back, because Australians love a bad boy.

The *Sun-Herald*'s David Sygall adds Johns' name to a list of bad boys who've all made a comeback, including Shane Warne, Andrew Symonds, Wendell Sailor and Ben Cousins. And he quotes sociologist David Rowe, of the University of Western Sydney, who believes that Johns has considerable public support: 'It might look like a boundary was crossed following the *Four Corners* program, yet there's still ambivalence about this behaviour from many people.' Indeed, Australian Defence Force Academy sociologist, James Connor, thinks Matthew Johns will follow his brother back into the fold. Once his playing career was over, Andrew Johns, also a rugby league star and a regular media commentator for the Nine Network, confessed to an addiction to drugs. The penitent was rewarded for his honesty by being restored to the public's favour. '[T]he same media strategy is being used for [Matthew] as was used for his brother', said Connor, 'They'll take him off the radar for a few months and slowly put him back on as people conveniently "forget". There will be the line about him being contrite, that he's a reformed sinner.'[22]

To Nine's credit it did try in 2005 to introduce a woman onto the panel of the *Footy Show*. But sports journalist Rebecca Wilson lasted exactly one week. Fatty Vautin and co-host Peter Sterling put their foot down. The Network's culture represents something male and swaggeringly combative. Men like Steve Roach and Matthew Johns may be nice blokes, but they're also strong, don't-give-a-shit types who behave in a blokey, in-your-face way. Nine doesn't condone bad behaviour, but it is loyal to its people. It's not into niceness, however: it's a business and there's no money in polishing plastic. Unless it's a credit card. It's just a pity that there is not more room in its culture for the sensitivity expressed by David Gyngell when he made the Network's apology to the traumatised young New Zealander.

A network is more than its owner, or its board, or general manager or network executives, but not much more. These are the people who set the style, the tone and the culture of the organisation. Perhaps the Nine Network needs to drop the testosterone levels in the coffee of its management. With the future of commercial television dependent on its relationship with the broader community, perhaps it's time to let go of those more old-fashioned views and attitudes. There may still be strong audiences for the *Footy Show*'s brand of boozy, misogynistic humour. However, if this only brings them high ratings, then the message they give out is clear: we have no responsibility, we leave that to others. The fact is, broadcasters do have a responsibility and it's not about the morality of nudity or bad language, it's about the human value we place on individuals and relationships. That comes with the licence.

7

Down the
Futurescope

Three things are certain about the future of television. It won't be the same. It will be the same. It won't go away.

Over the last thirty years, the innovations made in television's technical abilities have been impressive. While not exactly the knowledge of gods, television aspires to a god's-eye view. Mounted in interplanetary spacecraft or cricket stumps, or in capsules that can be swallowed deep inside the human body, the camera is already pretty-well all-seeing. Little wonder that the human appetite for pictures over words is stronger than ever. That's unlikely to change.

The technology to render an image on a screen is approaching the sophistication of the human eye. High-definition digital television is almost clinical in its rendition and we shall soon be able to install it on our ceilings. Japanese scientists, it appears, 'are developing a wallpaper that can be turned into a TV screen with the help of nanotechnology. As well as being able to turn entire walls into a screen, the flexible paper can be adjusted to show images to suit your mood.'[23] Moreover, we can expect to view the world with television technologies that will have achieved the ultimate in portability. Universal signal access will mean unlimited mobility. And these technological 'advances' will be accompanied by an enormous increase in viewer choices. Before long every major multi-platform service provider will be able to hold the individual preferences and viewing history of every subscriber. That will mean nothing less than programs on demand: the subscriber will be able to watch anything, anywhere, at anytime. Watching episode 8 of *Fawlty Towers* at 2.16 on a Saturday morning, in the carpark in the Olgas, will be a simple matter of booking the request.

On 27 April 2009, the Ten Network announced it would not be persisting with its 20-year relationship with *The Simpsons*. Payments of $25k per episode could not be maintained in tough economic times. This is part of a long-term trend. There is little doubt that all around the world the audience for free-to-air television is steadily diminishing. In the last three years it has decreased by 6.6 per cent. More alarming is that the young demographic sector of 15–25-year-old viewers has decreased by 7.6 per cent. Clearly, competition from the internet, pay television and electronic games is taking its toll.

Experience overseas shows that commercial free-to-air networks are in a long-term struggle which will weaken their audience base and tax their ability to survive. It's hard to raise cash during a global financial crisis. With each of the Australian commercial networks carrying significant debts, it's critical for them to maintain market share (i.e. ratings) because it is that which determines how much they can charge their advertisers. To that end, the Nine Network set out in

2006 to prevent a small media company, electronic program provider (EPG) IceTV, from copying station programming schedules. Publicly, Nine maintained that these schedules are material covered by copyright. The real issue was that the Network did not want their schedules used in any EPG technology that would allow viewers to navigate the schedules for themselves, and to select and record programs for later viewing. Giving more choice and control to the viewers meant that the Network would no longer be able to guarantee to its advertisers that the promised audience would be watching their commercials at the time intended. In the landmark 'David and Goliath battle', that ran to three years of appeals, counter appeals and millions of dollars in legal fees, the High Court finally ruled in favour of IceTV, 'a blow to efforts by [the Nine Network] to impose tighter controls on viewers'.[24]

The fight to maintain market share continues on all fronts, no matter how insignificant. On 9 March 2009, the ABC's *Media Watch* announced that Shannon Marinko and Lee Zachariah, two presenters of *The Bazura Project*, a comedy show about movies on Channel 31, were not eligible to be nominated for any of the fifty-first *TV Week* Logie Awards. Channel 31 is a community television station, and *The Bazura Project* is essential viewing for a small but devoted audience in Sydney, Melbourne, Brisbane and Adelaide. *TV Week* is a wholly-owned subsidiary of PBL Media, which also owns the Nine Network. Despite the rules covering the Logies, which allowed an entry from Marinko and Zachariah, Cate Carpenter, project manager of the awards, rejected *The Bazura Project* because,

'TV WEEK's decision is to not accept submissions from community TV'.[25] Every little helps.

Since the 1980s the profits generated by commercial networks have been eaten up by competition from other media and substantial interest payments. The most effective means of ensuring a healthy bottom line is to cut production costs. So-called 'reality TV' offers financial benefits because costs are limited to franchise rights and a host or two; there are no screenwriters or actors to pay. According to John Hartley, people like to cast their vote:

> The yoking together of politics and entertainment is as old as democracy itself. What is new is a shift from 'modern' democratic processes to a new paradigm based not on representation but on direct participation; a shift led from consumer rather than from political culture.

Hartley calls this interface between consumers and popular media 'plebiscitary industries' and defines them as 'those agencies, production companies, and technical service providers whose business it is to commercialize the popular vote by turning it into an entertainment format.'[26]

In the early 1970s the BBC conducted an experiment to find out what people did while they watched TV. Installed in the sets of consenting households, video cameras recorded everything in the living room from the moment the television was switched on. It didn't take long for the BBC to start having misgivings: viewers began to perform for the camera, having arguments, even having sex. Thirty years before the Dutch company, Endemol, franchised the idea, this was the prototype for *Big Brother*. In 2000 Neil Balnaves's Australian production house Southern Star formed a joint venture with Endemol and acquired *Big Brother*. It was a timely move, for Southern Star's fortunes were not in the ascendant. The show rated through the roof. When asked about the show's social value, Balnaves replied: 'It gives people windows into other people's lives and stopped people being isolated.'[27] For Hartley there is more to it than that. In his view *Big Brother* is 'the purest of the reality TV plebiscites, because viewers vote for (or rather against) contestants on the basis of what Martin Luther King Jr called the content of their character. Musical or other talents, no matter how dubious, are not the criteria for survival or success.'[28]

Since the late 1960s, television has attempted to diversify, offering more choice, and yet it has still fallen back to earth with game shows, reworked cop and hospital shows, and 'reality' series. By the 1990s big-budget 'event' television in the United States had increasingly become the province of subscriber networks which have the power to recoup their production outlays through advertising and repeat broadcasts. But it's difficult to imagine that Hartley's 'plebiscitary industries' are going to disappear. While Neil Balnaves has made a small fortune out of 'stopping people being isolated', the fact is that *Big Brother* was conceived as a 'multi-platform' production, a money-spinner for which the audience is made to pay twice. Evidence that Hartley is correct in believing that people like to vote can be found in the vast sums of money that Endemol and the Ten Network rake in from call charges make by viewers voting for 'evictions from the house'. Perhaps governments around the world could profit from a strategy of making voting easy and charging for it?

For viewers, the big question, the one that's worth asking, is, will the content improve? Well, according to Marshall McLuhan, that doesn't matter. But in the land of the living it does matter, a great deal. If the present trend of gradually diminishing world audiences continues, however, how will it affect television in Australia? In a surprising way, it will have a direct impact on the fight to maintain our cultural diversity. Commercial free-to-air networks have generally been very profitable. The Nine and Seven Networks have enjoyed high profit margins. And despite suffering several changes of ownership, the Ten Network manages to keep its head above water. All three, however, labour under burdens of debt, which keep them keen to run their operations lean. Nonetheless, if audiences continue to decrease, advertisers will, understandably, diversify their budgets and include other outlets for their message. Every cent that goes into website, mobile, game and DVD media advertising is a cent lost to free-to-air.

The economic pressures on both public and commercial broadcasting, pressures that have increased over the last two decades, have left the issue of culture to struggle on in academic circles and other places where the arts are discussed. Ratings don't mean quality. And often, for commercial interests, ratings are the only measure that matters. The challenge for all broadcasters facing an uncertain future is to maintain their economic viability, while protecting their cultural relevance. And that means *not* ignoring quality.

The Australian Government introduced content quotas for television in the early 1960s. Commercial networks must produce a minimum of 55 per cent of their total programming in Australia. Pay-TV has it easier. Only 10 per cent of its drama budget needs to be spent in Australia. Content quotas have been the cause of much heartache. Almost fifty years later, the commercial networks and Pay-TV continue to kick against the requirement. The reason for a content quota is simple. Without them, Australian television audiences would be overwhelmed by overseas product. Currently the going price for an hour of high-quality drama made in Australia is about $1m. To purchase drama made overseas costs between $50,000 and $80,000. Australians like watching local drama, but, as Franco Papandrea points out, some networks have only one priority: 'The Seven Network's success with the broadcast of Australian drama in excess of quota obligations and the apparent difficulties of the Nine Network in complying with the quota.'[29]

Mortified is a children's television series, created by one of Australia's most gifted writers, the late Angela Webber. Commissioned by the Nine Network in 2004, it soon attracted the willing participation of the BBC, who liked it so much that they commissioned two 13-part series and offered themselves as co-production partners. The Nine Network Drama Department, led by Posie Graeme-Evan and Jo Horsburgh, were enthusiastic from the start and their faith was not misplaced. *Mortified* was finished on schedule and on budget, and it delighted viewers. During the course of 2006–07, the series, individual episodes, the series writer, director and young actors all earned awards and accolades (ATOM, AFI and *TV Week* Logie awards) here in Australia. It won even more overseas, in the USA (CHRIS awards, Chicago International Children's Film Festival, New York Festival, US International Film and Video Festival), in Canada (Banff World Television Awards), in Korea (Seoul Drama Awards), and in Bulgaria (Golden Chest Awards). Most recently, in 2008 it won a bronze medal at the Cairo International Film Festival, and at the Prix Jeunesse International Festival it was voted the program (in all categories) that represented gender in the most positive way.[30]

In a word, *Mortified* delighted everyone who saw it—everyone, that is, except the Nine Network management, who chose to treat its own production as an orphan. The Network chose not to make a single promotional clip, place a single advertisement or let a potential audience know the series even existed. So, why would the network turn its back on a program of which they should have been justly proud? Is it because children's programming isn't subject to ratings? A leading producer of both children's and adult drama explained it this way:

> As far as I know, ratings are measured throughout the day, so I don't think it's to do with that specifically. I think there are two factors. Firstly, the cost of making the shows is generally higher than the advertising revenue, so they resent being forced to make it. And secondly, they want to demonstrate to government that children aren't watching the shows, so the quota isn't working, so they shouldn't

have to do it. It's one of those circular arguments that can really do your head in if you think about it, i.e. if they promoted them more, then more children would know about it, the ratings would go up, and then they might get better advertising (especially if they were sensible about promoting via the internet). Most children's projects commissioned by [...] independent producers are dramas, because they have a quota requirement to produce a minimum of 32 hours of first-run children's drama a year. Children's drama is fairly expensive to make (often as much as adult drama and more restrictive working conditions), and it usually has to work internationally to get financed. So financing involves several overseas partners (always expensive). Also, for the producer to secure Screen Australia investment, there's a floor price of $95,000 per half-hour from the networks (which could still be only 25 per cent of the budget). For the networks, they would probably never get that amount covered by advertising revenue during the afternoon. So it costs them money. The government sees it as part of their licence requirement, but the networks keep pushing to get it changed.[31]

Mortified was used by the network to satisfy its obligations under the Australian content quota regulations. Nine ran the series over two ratings periods in order to maximise its credits. When the BBC came back with an offer to co-finance another series, it was rejected. It would seem that the Nine Network sees success as something to avoid, perhaps because it serves to strengthen the regulator's hand.

8

The Buddha's Station

In June 1999, on the occasion of the 25th anniversary of his coronation, Bhutan's King Jigme Singye Wangchuck decreed that his people should have television. He consulted with Buddhist monks in his kingdom and a number of overseas media experts and it was decided that the only way the influence of the outside world could be tempered was by the creation of a public broadcasting channel, the Bhutan Broadcasting Service.

The mandate of this Himalayan kingdom's broadcaster would be to strengthen the Bhutanese's sense of identity in the face of an inevitable cultural onslaught from the outside world. To combat the commercial hard sell, the faces and feelings of Bhutan's 800,000 Buddhists should be seen to convey something more; the lights, the sinews of culture. It was for this purpose that the Bhutan Broadcasting Service was set up. Three months after the public broadcaster threw the switch to vaudeville, those who could afford TV sets signed up to receive another 45 channels, most of them from Rupert Murdoch's Star TV network.[32]

When a developing country begins television broadcasting, the licences are auctioned off, the transmitters go up and the advertising juices set about whetting the appetite of the masses. Did all those glazed faces basking in the cold light of television screens in mountain huts and rural villages wonder if they had just chained themselves to an engine for stimulating growth? As the world swept in, perhaps they thought of the industrial age welling up like a tsunami not far over the horizon. How long would it be before factories and billboards would darken the sky and everyone would be working and consuming to keep the monster alive? But that didn't happen. The only factories were the ones seen on TV. What did happen was more complicated and longer-lasting.

About one third of the population purchased a set within the first year. The changes weren't long in coming: from the rearrangement of furniture to accommodate the television set to the end of dinner conversation as the family stared and ate before the magic of those 45 channels. Parents confessed that they'd rather talk TV than talk to their kids. Young women wanted paler skin. Young men started to adopt American-brand clothing.

In April 2002, Bhutan experienced its first crime wave. In that one month the police laid charges for two murders, ancient stupas vandalised and robbed, bashings and embezzlement. The public broadcasting entity, BBS, was not the cultural influence that had been hoped for. The Minister for Health and Education, Sangay Ngedup, knew where the trouble was coming from: 'Until recently, we shied away from killing insects, and yet now we Bhutanese are asked to watch people on TV blowing heads off with shotguns. Will we now be blowing each other's heads off?' His frustration over the changes in Bhutanese society revolved around the public broadcaster: 'You can never predict the impact of things like TV or the urbanisation it brings with it. But you can prepare. If the BBS was intended as our answer to the cable world, I have to say that, at the moment, it is rather pathetic.'[33] Not everyone was as pessimistic as Sangay Ngedup, however; Mynak Tulku, the reincarnation of a powerful lama and the King's unofficial ambassador for new technology, was more optimistic than his Minister:

> I am so excited about technology, and let me tell you that TV's OK, as long as you appreciate that it is a transitory experience. I tell my students that it's like rushing in from the cold, going straight to the heater and ending up with frostbite. Ha, ha. TV can make you think that you are being educated, when in fact all you're doing is blinking your life away with a remote control. Ha, ha.[34]

By 2004, however, the writing was on the wall. The Bhutanese government began to seriously consider the regulation of broadcasting. In its haste to introduce television it had failed to set up a classification board or lay down regulations regarding media ownership. The cable operators had exercised no restraint in broadcasting whatever they wanted. In a proposed Information, Communication and Technology Act it was thought that the programs most likely to be taken off air would include pornography and staged US wrestling programs.[35] There was evidence that the level of violence in the schoolyard was increasing. Dorji Penjore, a government researcher, blamed television:

> Even my children are changing. They are fighting in the playground, imitating techniques they see

on World Wrestling Federation. Some have already been injured, as they do not understand that what they see is not real. When I was growing up, WWF meant World Wide Fund for Nature.[36]

Last year, Bhutan had its first election. Television played an important part in arranging the issues and candidates before the people. Throughout Bhutan, there is an ongoing conversation about the need for regulation and content quotas. Many are putting their faith in a stronger public broadcaster to counteract the influence from across their borders. Very few even contemplate turning back the clock. Television is here to stay and in a Buddhist way they have decided they must learn to deal with it. It is after all, the way the world works. The High Lama, Mynak Tulku, decided to take the long way: 'Change is not to be feared, without choice you cannot choose the right path.'[37]

Endnotes

1 See R.W. Burns, *Television: An International History of the Formative Years* (London: Institution of Electrical Engineers, 1998).

2 The patent application, 'Radioskop', was added to UNESCO's Memory of the World program in 2001.

3 See Frank Dixon, *Inside the ABC: A Piece of Australian History* (Melbourne: Hawthorn Press, 1975).

4 See Gerald Stone, *Who Killed Channel 9?: The Death of Kerry Packer's Mighty TV Dream Machine* (Sydney: Pan Macmillan, 2007).

5 See www.cultureandrecreation.gov.au/wsd/6531.htm (accessed 17 May 2009).

6 *Washington Post*, 24 November 2002.

7 BBC, *Ascent of Man*, 1973.

8 'Re-thinking Information and Communications Technology Policy Focus on Internet versus Teledensity Diffusion for Africa's Least Developed Countries', *Electronic Journal of Information Systems in Developing Countries*, 9 (2002).

9 *Understanding Media: The Extensions of Man* (New York: Mentor, 1964), pp. 8–9.

10 *Television Truths: Forms of Knowledge in Popular Culture* (London: Wiley-Blackwell, 2007), p. 73.

11 See Seth Mydans, 'The Police Verdict: Los Angeles Policemen Acquitted in Taped Beating', *New York Times*, 30 April 1992.

12 *Official Negligence: How Rodney King and the Riots Changed Los Angeles and the LAPD* (New York: Perseus, 1999).

13 'Unanimous Verdict in Democracy Divided', *Sydney Morning Herald*, 22 August 2006.

14 *Ibid.*

15 *Sunday Times*, 18 January 2009.

16 *Sydney Morning Herald*, 2 March 2009.

17 *Sydney Morning Herald*, 4 May 2009.

18 Robyn Ironside, *Courier Mail*, 27 April 2009.

19 Australian Writers' Guild, *Storyline*, 22 (Autumn 2008).

20 Text transcribed from www.youtube.com/watch?v=6L-TRnYLPuk (accessed 21 May 2009).

21 *Sydney Morning Herald*, 6 May 2007.

22 *Sun-Herald*, 17 May 2009.

23 'Wallpaper TV in the Pipeline', *Sydney Morning Herald*, 25 February 2009.

24 *Sydney Morning Herald*, 22 April 2009.

25 Transcript of *Media Watch*, ABC-TV, 9 March 2009.

26 *Television Truths*, p. 149.

27 *Sydney Morning Herald*, 23 March 2009.

28 *Television Truths*, p. 148.

29 'Improving Regulation of the Domestic Content of Australian Television', *Agenda*, 4: 4 (1997), 455–64.

30 Details courtesy of the Australian Childrens' Television Foundation.

31 Independent Australian producer (name withheld).

32 Cathy Scott-Clark & Adrian Levy, 'Fast Forward into Trouble', *Guardian*, 14 June 2003.

33 *Ibid.*

34 *Ibid.*

35 *BBC News*, 17 June 2004.

36 Cathy Scott-Clark & Adrian Levy, *op.cit.*

37 *BBC News*, 19 June 2004.

Readers' Forum

Response to Hilary Glow and Katya Johanson's *Your Genre is Black: Indigenous Arts and Policy.*

Andrea James is a graduate of La Trobe University and the Victorian College of the Arts, a playright and theatre director, author of *Yanagai! Yanagai!* (2003). At present she is Community Arts Worker at the Koorie Heritage Trust, Melbourne and she was a speaker at the public forum held on 10 February 2009.

They call me a mid-career artist, a writer and director of Indigenous descent with a spattering of productions under my belt. But having just absorbed the new Platform Paper and the Australia Council document. 'Love Your Work: training, retaining and connecting artists in theatre', I can't help but feel that as a theatre practitioner with over ten years' experience, I've been put on the scrap heap. Along with a whole host of other, just as experienced and talented, Indigenous theatre-makers: Kylie Belling, Johnny Harding, Jane Harrison, Tammy Anderson—just to name a few.

According to the Australia Council figures, I have about forty opportunities to direct for the mainstage. Out of these, about ten or 15 will go to directors who are making the transition from small-medium to mainstage. About *two* will be Indigenous—Wesley Enoch and Wayne Blair over the last few years. I cannot recall a single situation where an Indigenous female theatre director has made it into directing a *mainstage* theatre show. Though there may be one. It is a very tough glass ceiling to crack into.

Writers in particular get a great show up and then disappear. No mainstream companies want to take the risk to produce our new work, except for maybe Belvoir Street and the Melbourne Workers Theatre (which has now lost federal funding and is on the brink of collapse).

This is an appeal to the policy makers and those in our community who have the power to direct policy and resources. The state of Indigenous theatre and the livelihoods of some of our most talented Indigenous theatre-makers are at stake. As is the Australian theatre environment.

Indigenous theatre has laid the groundwork for great change, particularly in the 1980s and '90s. We reflected the political and social changes that happened in our communities and we celebrated them in performance. We have drawn out the issues that all Australians needed to hear. We made them palatable, entertaining and challenging. We moved people to laughter, to tears and sometimes into action. We engendered pride and strength in Aboriginal communities. We put our cousins and brothers and sisters and aunties and uncles on the stage and people were proud of us. And now it seems that the community we so supported has turned its back on us. Black and white alike.

This is a plea. And I don't want to be melodramatic, but unless we put resources into Indigenous performance, the place for our stories, culture and language will diminish. There is no other place where the true spirit of ceremony, performance and language can be expressed. Film just doesn't cut it. Through performance we re-inhabit, and make sacred again, space, ceremony and culture.

Another issue: no land, no ceremony, no culture. Without theatre spaces and venues we can't survive. It's like trying to do important ceremony when there's no land. It's like being put into a home and locked out of the yard. There's Tandanya (the Indigenous visual arts centre in Adelaide), there's Bunjilaka (the Museum of Victoria's Indigenous cultural centre) and there's Koorie Heritage Trust—with plans afoot to relocate and incorporate a performance space into a new venue.

At present we lack trained Indigenous people in the industry. Without people trained as theatre-makers, actors, designers, directors, writers and theatre managers we cannot make our art; and Indigenous culture, language, stories will diminish. Australia has only one Indigenous theatre course, in Brisbane. Swinburne has closed down. There are some access policies in WAAPA, VCA and NIDA, and a few Indigenous artists get through.

As Glow and Johanson point out, for too long Indigenous theatre-makers have carried a double function. As well as being expected to knock out fantastic theatre, we had to be community-development workers and statisticians. And that's okay. We all want to work for and with our communities. But it has come at the cost of the quality of our theatre and the presentation of good art and culture. We are artists. It's time to rebalance this, to put the community and social issues aside and focus on art and culture. And I believe this will not come at the expense of the Indigenous Community. To resource and mentor top-quality theatre practitioners makes for good theatre, which makes for good representation and stronger communities. Regardless of whether arts funding and policy has a social, community or artistic agenda, Indigenous artists are, and will forever be, a part of their community—even when we choose to work in mainstream productions or with mainstream companies. It is possible for us to have a leg in both camps and now it is time to nurture the art form, to embrace live performance as a place for new high-quality art and the expression of ceremony and culture.

As Indigenous theatre-makers we need to experiment, we need to fail.

Where is the avant-garde in Indigenous theatre? We see this in the visual arts with Tracey Moffatt and Christian Thompson, but not in the theatre. We need to reflect the current trend, which is away from text-based theatre and towards visual and movement-based forms. This is something that we have done traditionally. But lately there has been a proliferation of text-based work and this really does need to shift. But to develop this we need the training and the experience and the appreciation of non-naturalistic art.

To end my plea on a positive note, I say this to the policy makers: Indigenous artists will continue to make art no matter what. Our will and desire to create and tell stories and work with others are strong. We do this almost despite ourselves. My work for the Koorie Heritage Trust has shown me that there are Indigenous people making art all over the state. It is dynamic and varied and prolific, despite the lack of resources. We need to channel policy, energy and funds into Indigenous art across all art forms.

Here is a wish list and some possible solutions

1. An Indigenous theatre company and Indigenous theatre training course *in each state* and with a mixture of urban- and regionally-based companies.
2. A national mainstage theatre company based in Melbourne that takes good work to the next level, tours

it nationally and internationally and puts practitioners into a mainstage setting so that we do not stay forever in the small-to-medium sector but have a chance to develop our careers and become a theatre elder.

3. Indigenous theatre traineeships and cadetships, like those offered in the community for health workers, lawyers and cultural officers. The Sand-to-Celluloid Series, out of the Australian Film Institute, has produced so many great Indigenous filmmakers and could be a model for the theatre sector.

Mainstream theatre institutions must take responsibility for providing emerging and established Indigenous artists with real opportunities. The few fledging Indigenous theatre companies around Australia are fast disappearing: Ilbijerri, Kooemba Jdarra are gone, Yirra Yaakin has lost funding and can't keep us in active work.

Finally, one model for us all to consider. You don't have to be a theatre or art institution to actively engage in art and theatre in everyday life. Bev Murray's artists-in-residence scheme at the Aboriginal Housing Board, provides a model and deserves acknowledgement. We must act now or the very heart and soul of our culture—that is storytelling and ceremony—will be lost forever.

Response to Robert Walker's *Beethoven or Britney? The Great Divide in Music Education*

Dr Richard Letts, AM, is founder and executive director the Music Council of Australia and is president of the International Music Council, based in Paris.

Bob Walker's paper is structured around the National Review of School Music Education, published in 2005, and mouldering since. The National Review is the most recent in a succession of studies going back to the late

'60s. That none of them had any substantial effect can be seen by the situation that Bob describes.

Bob writes of inadequate resources and contrasts the provisions made by some independent schools with those of the public systems. In fact, the Music Council has statistics that show that 88% of independent non-Catholic schools offer a competently-delivered music education, compared with 22% of public schools. That is a phenomenal inequity: 2 in 10 versus 9 in 10.

Isn't it interesting that the independent schools do this despite the fact that for it to be possible, parents must pay more? Apparently this is not a grudging payment, because music is a strong element in the marketing by these schools. Most offer general scholarships and then, next in number, music scholarships. The music offering is a point of differentiation with public schools, and, as Bob writes, probably a major attractor for the continuing switch from public to private.

Interestingly, in a regular attitudes-survey conducted by the Australian Music Association, 88%—that number again—88% of parents believe that all students should have the opportunity to study music at school. Ninety-four per cent of high-school students agree. The trouble is that most of those parents depend upon unwilling governments to make this possible.

Since governments don't want to pay for specialist music teachers, primary school music teaching is assigned to the classroom generalist teacher. On average, these student teachers receive 23 hours of instruction in music and music pedagogy over their four-year course. On this basis, they are then supposed to teach music all year at any of seven grade levels. If you gave your children 23 piano lessons, how much would you expect them to know?

Apparently the amount of instruction is entirely the prerogative of the universities. But there is little check on what the universities are producing. It seems that the state education departments do not require any evidence of subject-area competency. In NSW, applicants for primary-school positions are not asked about their competencies in any subject. They simply have to show that they have the degree. In NSW, there is a mandatory music curriculum for grades 1–6 but the Department has no idea whether its teachers are capable of delivering it and doesn't even want to find out. It's bizarre.

OK, crunch time. Let's get to Britney versus Beethoven.

Bob is saying that a serious music education will be one in Western classical music. 'Playing around with pop music' is not really a music education at all. This is not, says Bob, because Western classical music is superior; it's just that it embodies the depth and breadth of the history of Western civilisation. And pop music doesn't. In fact, pop is perpetrated by musicians who are only interested in money. 'Yet so powerful has been the intrusion of the Western arts music traditions into pop/rock, that most fans believe this music can also express feelings, emotions, and psychological states as powerfully as any operatic aria.' Are you confused, too?

My guess is that most fans would have little idea of the emotional content of an operatic aria. On the other hand, they would know whether the rock music causes them to feel emotions. Emotions as profound as you might feel listening to opera? I don't know. Does Bob?

A new survey of a thousand UK 15–24 year-olds found that 60% would rather go without sex than music for a week. That is a powerful statistic. There is something in their experience of pop and rock that goes pretty deep.

Nevertheless, I'm actually with the real Bob. Classical music is superior. All musics are equal? That's crap. Shakespeare was brilliant, but what would have been the outcome if he could work only with pidgin English? Classical music is superior not because of Pythagorean hocus-pocus, but because it has an extremely rich language, it is complex, flexible, powerful, capable of carrying a great range of subtle meanings and emotions. And it wasn't all written last week.

The question here is, when and in what circumstances should it be taught?

Bob says that pop music has taken over the curriculum because of the unfortunate triumph of socio-political theory over musical content. But I think the theory just gives a little validation to something quite different. What I have heard from some school music teachers is that their kids don't like classical music, and do love pop music. The teachers were tired of hurling themselves at the stone wall of student indifference and preferred to teach something the kids like. Indeed, are passionate about. And surely that's a fundamental thing about music. It's something to be passionate about. Everything starts from there.

As to musical content, the content of a good pop song can be comparable to the content of a classical song at the level for which young students are ready. After all, Bob has told us that the Western classical tradition has powerfully intruded on pop/rock.

If, when and how a kid comes to classical music depends firstly on whether there was classical music in the home. Then on education's need to create and sustain a passion for music-making. A good teacher, properly resourced, can awaken a passion for classical music where none existed. They can also include popular music as a vehicle for an effective music education. The big missing ingredient is, as usual, a commitment from most (but not all) governments to employ and support such teachers.

This is an extract from Dr Letts' speech at a Currency House forum on music education held at Sydney Grammar School on 6 May 2009.

Subscribe to **Platform Papers**

Have the papers delivered quarterly to your door

4 issues for $60.00 including postage within Australia

The individual recommended retail price is $14.95.

___ I would like to subscribe to 4 issues of Platform Papers for $60.00

I would like my subscription to start from: ___ this issue (No. 21)

___ the next issue (No. 22)

Name_____

Address_____

_____

_____ State _____ Postcode _____

Email _____

Telephone _____

Please make cheques payable to Currency House Inc.

Or charge: ___ Mastercard ___ Visa

Card no. ___ ___ ___ ___ ___ ___ ___ ___ ___ ___ ___ ___

___ ___ ___ ___

Expiry date _____ Signature _____

Fax this form to Currency House Inc. at: 02 9319 3649

Or post to: Currency House Inc., PO Box 2270,
Strawberry Hills NSW 2012 Australia

CURRENCY HOUSE